D0432208

COLLEGE FOOTBALL

TRADITIONS AND RIVALRIES

Chants, Pranks, and Pageantry

MORROW GIFT

An Imprint of HarperCollinsPublishers

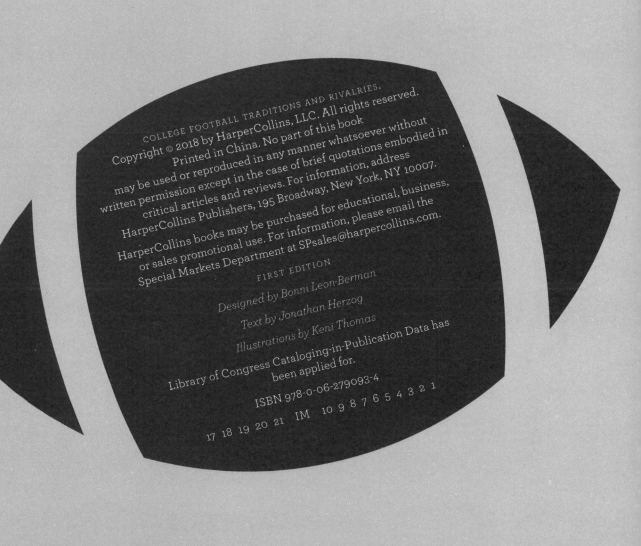

FIRST EDITION

Designed by Bonni Leon-Berman

Text by Jonathan Herzog

Illustrations by Keni Thomas

Library of Congress Cataloging-in-Publication Data has
been applied for.

ISBN 978-0-06-279093-4

17 18 19 20 21 IM 10 9 8 7 6 5 4 3 2 1

Introduction

Every fall, college football fans across the nation flock to their bleachers and big screens a ike to revel in joyous celebration of America's favorite sport. We don't just love the sport though, college football is about so much more. It's tailgating with our best friends and our families. It's about watching the bright young players greeting fans as they jog together into the stadium. It's about the thundering drums and the brassy horns in the band. It's about the traditions that bring us together—the ridiculous, the solemn, the extraordinary.

Each college campus has their own traditions exclusive to football season. Lots of schools made it into this book, but plenty also did not. We tried to get a representative number from every conference, knowing that ultimately even the schools you love to hate have a place in your heart. And to that end, we were sure to cover some of the sport's most contentious rivalries in the spirit of competition.

This book is for every college football fan: for the one who rolls out of their RV at 5 A.M. to start the grill for the best tailgate at the stadium, for the one who holds their friend on top of the crowd to do pushups, for the one at their first game just starting to fall in love with the thrill of the gridiron—cheer loudly!

You're what makes this game great.

TRADITIONS

Mr. Two Bits
UNIVERSITY OF FLORIDA

Every Gator fan worth two bits knows the Two Bits cheer, though real superfans know it originated with George Edmonson in 1949.

Back then, the Gators weren't the strongest gridiron competitors, ranking tenth out of twelve teams in the Southeastern Conference. Edmonson couldn't stand to see his beloved Florida team get booed by disheartened fans, and after the Gators made a fumble, George stood up and led the Two Bits cheer among his friends sitting nearby at the stadium.

Over time, other fans caught on and the tradition grew to include whole sections of Florida fans in Ben Hill Griffin Stadium. The university even caught on, and added Edmonson to official gameday festivities. He would head down onto the field before each home game to lead the whole crowd in his trademark cheer.

Trotting out on the field in his signature outfit—a bright-yellow dress shirt, seersucker pants, and an orange and blue tie—Edmonson would hold up his "2-BITS" sign and then start the crowd chanting, "Two Bits! Four Bits! Six Bits! A dollar! All for the Gators! Stand up and holler!!" Each part of the cheer got a different full-body movement from Edmonson to emphasize the phrase.

George Edmonson officially retired as Mr. Two Bits in 2008 at the age of eighty-six. Since then, leading the Two Bits cheer has become the responsibility of Florida's mascot, Albert the Alligator, who is joined by an ever-rotating cast of famous University of Florida alumni, mostly from the world of sports.

Rocky Top
UNIVERSITY OF TENNESSEE

Even though it's not the official fight song at Tennessee, no other song is so deeply associated with the University than the country song "Rocky Top."

The song was a country hit in the early 1970s, and the Pride of the Southland Marching Band decided to add it to their halftime country music show on October 21, 1972, during a game against Alabama. "Rocky Top" was an immediate success and quickly became one of the most popular songs in marching band's repertoire.

Nowadays, Vols fans may hear "Rocky Top" played more than forty times per home game by the Pride of the Southland. The song is so often deployed during games that coaches from opposing teams have been rumored to use it during practices to fire up their players before a matchup against the Vols.

"Rocky Top" is so ingrained into University of Tennessee culture that any gathering of students, alums, or fans becomes an excuse to play the song. Even NFL star Peyton Manning—a former Tennessee quarterback himself—was known to dance around to it during Indianapolis Colts practices. That "Rocky Top" spirit just never leaves the heart of a Volunteer!

"Rocky Top, you'll always be home sweet home to me!"

Ringing the Chapel Bell
UNIVERSITY OF GEORGIA

The UGA Chapel Bell was originally crafted in 1832, housed in the tower of the UGA Chapel. In 1913, it was moved to its current location atop a wooden tower and was rung to signal the beginning and end of class periods.

Nowadays, access to the Chapel Bell's rope is available to everyone. The bell serves a wide range of purposes, as Bulldogs ring the Chapel Bell to mark personal milestones and academic achievements.

However, the most fun use of the Chapel Bell is in the wake of UGA football victories. Following a victory at home in Athens, Georgia, Bulldogs fans will race from the stadium to the bell to be the first to swing that rope and signal another victory for UGA. Bell-ringing will often go on for a long time, especially in the wake of a hard-fought victory or a triumph over a close rival.

The Kentucky Doubleheader
UNIVERSITY OF KENTUCKY

The state of Kentucky is famous for its horse racing, and because of some smart coordination between the University of Kentucky and a local racetrack, Wildcats fans can have their college football and their horse racing all in one day.

Kentucky plays all of their home games at night, so savvy Wildcats football fans do some of their tailgating during the day at the nearby Keeneland racetrack. The University even helps to provide shuttles back and forth from campus to the track, encouraging Wildcats fans to hit both attractions in one day.

Wildcats fans roll out of bed late on a Saturday, hop on a bus to the local track, maybe catch a future Kentucky Derby or Preakness winner in a race, and are back on campus by kickoff.

The locals call this both "The Keeneland-UK Double" or "The Kentucky Doubleheader." Regardless of its name, there's nothing quite like this anywhere but in Lexington.

Theme from *2001: A Space Odyssey*
UNIVERSITY OF SOUTH CAROLINA

Every college football team has an impressive entrance onto the field, but none may be more awe-inspiring than the entrance by the University of South Carolina Gamecocks.

The stadium announcers and cheerleaders get the crowd hyped up with chants of "Gamecocks! Gamecocks!" that fill the stadium with a deafening noise until the announcement comes over the speakers that "It's time for Carolina football!" and the crowd erupts with cheering.

Then, through the speakers, Gamecocks fans hear the opening lines of the song "Thus Spake Zarathustra," a classical composition by Richard Strauss that Stanley Kubrick famously used for the opening scene of his movie *2001: A Space Odyssey*. The climbing brass and explosive fanfare herald the entrance of Carolina's gridiron heroes, and the thundering timpani drums underscore the dread that their opponents should be feeling.

Small fireworks erupt from the field and the crowd's roaring reaches feverous levels by the time the third fanfare blasts through the speakers. Then the flag guard charges across the field with their Carolina banners, and the football players emerge from the locker room tunnel. The players dash across the field as the triumphant music peaks and Carolina is ready to play some football!

The Admiral

Just above the press box inside Vanderbilt Stadium rests The Admiral, a naval horn originally from a decommissioned United States Navy battleship. When the ship was being taken apart in 1993, its highest-ranking officer—a Vanderbilt alumnus—decided to salvage the ship's horn and donate it to his old alma mater.

Now every time the Vanderbilt Commodores score a touchdown, a member of the University's Naval ROTC sounds "the foghorn," releasing a deafening noise that blasts across Vanderbilt Stadium and drowning out the thunderous cheers of the fans.

Every time The Admiral makes that noise, Commodores fans know that it's good news for Vandy!

Truman's Taxi
UNIVERSITY OF MISSOURI

At every Mizzou home game, the marching band entertains Tigers fans with their outstanding pregame performance before the announcers introduce the starting lineup of the University of Missouri football team.

As this happens, a vintage fire truck from Boone County, Missouri, drives in front of the student section of the stadium flanked by cheerleaders. Hanging out atop the gorgeous, bright-yellow truck is Truman the Tiger, Mizzou's energetic feline mascot.

The crowd cheers wildly as Truman jumps around and dances his signature moves to reward them for their excitement. Truman even occasionally uses the old truck's hose to spray the students with water to cool them off before games!

After the announcer finishes introducing the players, Truman hops down and joins the rest of the pep squad to keep Mizzou's energy up for the game.

Rammer Jammer
UNIVERSITY OF ALABAMA

One of the most widely recognized cheers in all of college football is the University of Alabama's "Rammer Jammer."

At the conclusion of each victory, the band begins playing the taunting song and the other Crimson Tide fans single out their opponent by name. For example, when the Tide beats their bitter rivals, Auburn, 'Bama fans shout "Hey Auburn!" three times when cued by the band. These three callouts are followed by the rest of the cheer: "We just beat the hell out of you! Rammer Jammer! Yellowhammer! Give 'em hell, Alabama!!"

The cheer used to be played before each game to warn opponents of their impending defeat, but in the year 2000, the University leadership decided the unsportsmanlike cheer should no longer be played by the band. A few years later, students voted in a campus-wide referendum to keep the cheer tradition, and it was allowed to be played by the band following victories.

The University of Alabama has a long history of proud football traditions, but maybe the one that's truest to its fans is its proud celebration of victory. Roll Tide!

Rolling Toomer's Corners
AUBURN UNIVERSITY

At the edge of Auburn University's campus, where the college meets the town of Auburn, there is a small patch of ground named Toomer's Corners. It's here, at the corner of College Street and Magnolia Avenue, that Tigers fans meet to celebrate football victories.

Beneath the branches of the tall oak trees that stand at Toomer's corner, victory celebrations extend for hours after the football games have ended. Auburn fans from both the university and the town gather together to cheer and chant, revel and rejoice, but most important, to throw rolls of toilet paper. By the end of every victory celebration, each oak tree at Toomer's Corners is completely draped in white by Auburn fans.

The oaks at Toomer's Corners were also at the center of some controversy in January 2011 when an angry Alabama fan poisoned his rivals' treasured 130-year-old oak trees. The act was widely denounced by people on both side of the Alabama-Auburn rivalry; unfortunately the trees did not survive.

Since then, Auburn has revitalized and expanded Toomer's Corners, and new oaks were planted in 2015 and are standing strong today as evidence that Auburn's spirit is strong and runs deep!

"Touchdown for LSU"
LOUISIANA STATE UNIVERSITY

Most schools have pregame shows played by their marching bands, but a special history behind the music sets apart LSU's pregame show by The Golden Band from Tiger Land.

Back in the 1930s, Louisiana governor, senator, and famous populist Huey P. Long took a strong interest in his State University's football team. He was so invested in the success of the football program that he once strong-armed the Barnum and Bailey Circus to shut down their show when it was competing for ticket sales with an LSU Tigers game.

Governor Long also turned that attentive eye to the Golden Band from Tiger Land when he personally selected the new music director, Castro Carazo, for an overhaul of the band's sound and operations. Then, he did one better: he and Carazo co-wrote a song for the band to play called "Touchdown for LSU."

Each week when the band starts its pregame show with the song that goes, "Touchdown! Touchdown! It's Tigers score," they're playing a little bit of LSU and Louisiana history, courtesy of one of the Tigers' most ardent fans.

The 12th Man
TEXAS A&M UNIVERSITY

Many college and professional football programs have adopted the notion that the fanbase is truly the 12th man on the gridiron. This idea originated at Texas A&M.

Back in 1922, Texas A&M student E. King Gill had left the football team to focus on basketball instead, but his experience with the team and players made him a great resource up in the press box for reporters trying to identify players on the field during games. During the tough-fought Dixie Classic (a precursor to the Cotton Bowl), the Aggies faced a high number of injuries and coach D. X. Bible called on Gill to suit up and join the team on the sidelines.

When the game ended, the Aggies were victorious; Gill was the final player standing on the sidelines, still ready to play for his team. He said, "I simply stood by in case my team needed me."

Now all Aggies fans think of themselves as the 12th man—standing by to support the team, suited up for game day in maroon and white, and cheering their hearts out for the players on the field. This dedication to the team and the game of football is an Aggies tradition that's endured for years.

Calling the Hogs
UNIVERSITY OF ARKANSAS

The Arkansas Razorbacks certainly have a unique way of showing their support for their football team: treating them like pigs.

In a tradition that dates back to the 1920s, University of Arkansas football fans have been "Calling the Hogs" for almost a hundred years to show their favorite football team how much they love them.

The cheer is quite simple, just three repeats of "Woo! Pig! Sooie!" with a series of hand motions that go along with each part. Excited fans raise both arms over their heads, and while wiggling their fingers, they hold out a long "Woo!" Then, they drop their hands, make two fists, and shout, "Pig!" Last, each faithful Razorback fan punches a fist into the air and yells, "Sooie!" just like you would to call a pig home.

Opponents may scoff at Arkansas' country roots, but in a stadium filled with 100,000 enthusiastic Razorbacks fans cheering their team to victory, those long woos are deafening.

Sooie! Razorbacks!!

Cowbells

Ask anyone the number one thing they associate with Mississippi State football, and they'll say: cowbells.

Popular folklore around campus attributes the origin of this tradition to a game in the 1930s, when a cow wandered onto the football field on the day that State defeated rival Ole Miss. From that day forward, students would attempt to bring a cow to all games as a good luck charm, until the practice was changed to bringing the more portable cowbell instead.

As the cowbells became more widespread among the Bulldog fanbase, students decided they wanted an easier way to ring the cowbells, and turned to two Mississippi State professors: Earl Terrell and Ralph Reeves. These two industrious men came up with the idea of attaching a handle to the end of the bell and the practice spread very quickly.

The long-handled cowbell will be associated with Mississippi State football for all time. Whether the bell is plain or painted, whether it sports a Bulldog pawprint or a Mississippi State logo, whether the handle is a bicycle grip or an ornately carved bulldog, one thing is clear: the sound of a stadium full of Mississippi State Bulldogs fans clanging those cowbells is enough to cow their opponents.

The Grove
OLE MISS

Tailgating is as much of a part of college and professional football as the game itself! No matter what you eat or drink when you're tailgating for your favorite team, there's nowhere better for it than in The Grove at Ole Miss.

The Grove is ten full acres of campus real estate nestled beneath a canopy of oak and magnolia trees that provides a lovely traditional Southern tailgate setting for each home game at Ole Miss.

Rebels fans bring tents, excellent food, strong drinks, and their best red and blue attire to pre-party for each home game. The mood is friendly, fans mix and mingle from tent to tent, and everyone is made to feel welcome. There's an unwritten rule that no one is a stranger in The Grove and hospitality reigns supreme.

Tailgating in The Grove has gotten accolades as the best pre-football party spot from national media outlets like ESPN, *Sports Illustrated*, and the *New York Times*, but die-hard Ole Miss fans don't need all that attention to tell them how awesome The Grove is—they already know.

Guarding the Nittany Lion
PENN STATE

During Homecoming Week at Penn State, students out and about in the middle of the night probably aren't coming home from a late-night study session at the library. They may not even be coming from a party—chances are, they're coming from guarding the Nittany Lion Shrine.

The shrine is a statue of the Penn State mascot that was donated by the class of 1940, though the tradition of guarding the statue during Homecoming Week didn't actually start until the mid 1960s.

What prompted loyal Nittany Lions fans to guard their statue was actually an act of vandalism in 1966 by Sue Paterno, wife to Penn State's head coach. To get the student body excited for an upcoming game against Syracuse, she painted the beloved statue bright orange—Syracuse's color. Her ploy worked—the students were whipped into a frenzy for a few days, and the water-based paint was easily washed off.

However, some Syracuse students got wind of the prank and decided to paint the statue orange again, only they used an oil-based paint, which wasn't as easily removed.

Ever since, different student groups have taken turns guarding the statue all throughout Homecoming Week, sometimes taking shifts deep into the night. Now that's some Nittany Lion pride!

Dotting the "i"
OHIO STATE

The Pride of the Buckeyes Marching Band is something special. Rich in history, the band is considered pioneers in quite a few of the marching band innovations that most take for granted, such as animated field formations and script lettering.

The Pride of the Buckeyes are also one of the best college bands out there. For proof, check out their October 2013 tribute to Michael Jackson and try not to be impressed when the band forms a football-field-size version of the King of Pop and then makes it moonwalk.

Their best-known tradition is one that all Buckeyes fans look forward to at the start of each home game. The Ohio State band enters, and while playing "Le Regiment de Sambre-et-Meuse," the band performs their signature feat by literally signing the field with a giant script "Ohio."

The practice dates back to the 1930s when band director Eugene Weigel decided to add the feat into the band's repertoire. Led by the drum major, the entire band glides across the field in a single line like ink drawing out of a pen, all the way up to the dotting of the letter I.

As it's done now, one of the senior sousaphone players follows the drum major throughout the entire course of the word Ohio. Once the final O is formed, they high five and strut out to their place above the letter I. The drum major points and the sousaphone player assumes the spot as the dot on the letter. They then bow, and the crowd goes wild.

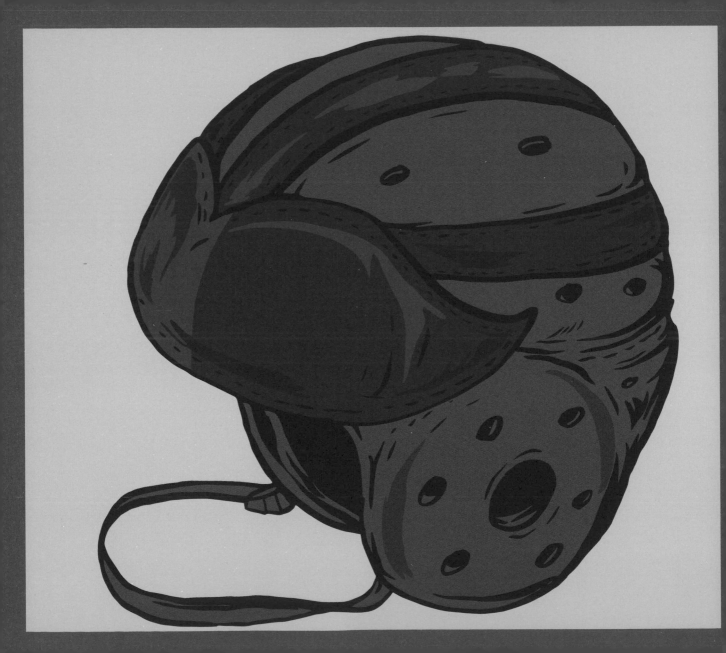

Winged Helmets
UNIVERSITY OF MICHIGAN

A dark-blue helmet streaked with bright maize-yellow stripes zipping down the football field is one of college athletics' most recognizable sights. When football fans see it, they instantly think of the University of Michigan, but only the most dedicated Wolverines fans know the history behind their team's distinct look.

When famed Michigan football coach Fritz Crisler came to campus in 1938, changing the look of the helmets was one of the first things that he did. He had used the now-famous "winged" helmet look at Princeton for the previous few years, and liked that the "wings" on the side provided extra protection for his players because of the extra layer of leather padding. Also, the three stripes running along the top of the helmets made his players more easily distinguished from the other team.

Though not the inventor of this design, as many people think, Crisler certainly helped to popularize it, and in doing so, left an indelible mark on Michigan's football program. Because the stripes and wings are used in the designs for other Michigan athletics teams as well, any Wolverine who has donned a jersey in the modern era has Crisler to thank for the look of their uniform.

Since his time as athletic director for the university, Fritz Crisler was honored with a reserved seat always left open for him at Michigan Stadium in Ann Arbor. Today, the official capacity of the stadium is 109,901 seats, with one seat always remaining empty in memory of Crisler and his enduring legacy.

Hep's Rock
UNIVERSITY OF INDIANA

At the northern end of Indiana's Memorial Stadium stands a fitting tribute to a coach who had a brief but lasting effect on the Hoosier football program.

Terry "Hep" Hoeppner came to Indiana after of a few successful seasons with Miami University in Ohio where he coached future NFL star Ben Roethlisberger to a Division 1-A championship in 2003.

Hep's goal was to build the team back up into a national competitor, and one of the ways he sought to do this was by building morale around "Hep's Rock." The rock is a huge boulder that Hep stumbled upon in the Hoosier practice field one day in 2005, during his first season as head coach. He ordered the white limestone boulder to be dug up, and then had it mounted onto a piece of granite and placed next to the northern end zone, right where the Hoosiers enter to start each home game.

As the team emerges from their locker room, each coach and player touches the rock as a show of strength and unity (and for a little good luck). Terry Hoeppner passed away in the spring of 2007 and the rock he placed inside Memorial Stadium was officially named Hep's Rock in his memory. At the end of the fall 2007 football season, the Indiana Hoosiers won a berth to their first bowl game in nearly fifteen years, though they lost in a competitive game to the Oklahoma State Cowboys.

To this day, each Hoosier player and coach touches the rock before coming out onto the field as a tribute to a man who never personally got to realize his vision for a dominant Indiana football program.

HEP'S ROCK

Zeke the Wonder Dog
MICHIGAN STATE

One of the halftime performers at Michigan State home games at Spartan Stadium in Lansing is doggone wonderful.

Back in 1977, the Spartans decided to try something new and brought yellow Lab and local Frisbee-catching champion Zeke the Wonder Dog to their games to entertain fans during halftime shows. After his introduction by the announcers, a neon-colored frisbee would zip down the field and Zeke would chase after it at lightning speed, snatching it out of the air with his powerful jaws. Even on the rare occasions when Zeke would miss, the crowd still went wild to see the famous canine leap into the air.

The original Zeke retired after wowing Michigan State until 1984, and for a number of years the Spartans went without a canine champion. Then, in 2002, the university decided to bring back this quirky and singular tradition, so Zeke II began his reign.

Today's incarnation of Zeke is a true Spartan celebrity. He hangs out with his adoring fans at tailgates and gets special VIP treatment at Spartan Stadium each Saturday that he's called on to show off his wondrous talents.

First Game Statue
RUTGERS UNIVERSITY

Rutgers University is one of the oldest colleges in the United States, and as such it's fitting that they were host to the very first intercollegiate football game.

On November 6, 1869, Rutgers and Princeton played, and the Scarlet Knights of Rutgers emerged victorious in a close matchup. However, the game followed rules that are widely different than college football today—players moved the ball down the field by kicking it, with no throwing or carrying allowed.

To commemorate this momentous day in sports history, Rutgers erected a statue in 1997 called *The First Football Game Monument* as a gift from the class of 1949. The bronze tribute stands just outside of High Point Solutions Stadium and greets Scarlet Knights fans to every home football game.

Before each game in New Brunswick, the Scarlet Knights walk down the red brick Scarlet Walk past crowds of fans ready to give a high five or handshake to their favorite players. Many schools do just this, but what makes Rutgers' tradition special is that each player also touches the first game statue on their way past.

Each player hopes that some of the luck that the Scarlet Knights had in that first victory will also be with them as they emerge from the locker room and take to the field today.

Jump Around
UNIVERSITY OF WISCONSIN

On October 10, 1998, the University of Wisconsin and Purdue were playing a tight game that was tied as the seconds ticked down to the end of the third quarter. With about 1:20 left on the clock, Purdue's quarterback Drew Brees threw an interception to Wisconsin defensive back Jamar Fletcher, who returned the ball 50 yards for a touchdown.

The feeling in the stadium was intense in the break between the third and fourth quarters at Camp Randall Stadium. When the song "Jump Around" by House of Pain played over the loudspeakers during the break, Wisconsin's student sections went crazy. They started jumping up and down on their bleachers and celebrating, and a new tradition was born.

The song has played between the third and fourth quarters of every home football game in Madison since. There's only one time that the song wasn't played: at the home opener in 2003 when the stadium was undergoing renovations.

The University of Wisconsin leadership was concerned that the stadium's structural integrity could be compromised by the Badgers' fans collective enthusiasm. This put the students in an uproar, so structural integrity tests were performed to the leadership's satisfaction, and the song was played the following Saturday.

This Badger tradition has spread to a few other schools, but no one will ever be able to match Wisconsin fans for their ability shake their stadium to its bones with their jumping!

The Pink Locker Room
UNIVERSITY OF IOWA

One of the most well-known destinations in college football is at Kinnick Stadium at the University of Iowa. But this spot isn't on the field or in the stands—it's in the visiting teams' locker room.

Back in 1979, when coach Hayden Fry had just arrived at Iowa, he was interested in improving the program by any means necessary (so long as it was within the rules and guidelines of the NCAA). And one of his strategies involved a bit of psychological warfare.

Fry heard about a study published that year by Alexander Schauss that showed painting rooms pink at the Naval correctional facility in Seattle had a calming effect on the prisoners kept in the pink holding cells, and that the researchers believed the long-term effects would also lower cardiovascular and strength performance. So Hayden Fry had his visitors' locker room painted pink in hopes it would make his opponents play poorly.

The pink locker room at Kinnick has not existed without creating controversy. Because Hayden Fry wrote in his autobiography that "some consider [pink] a sissy color," many University of Iowa professors, alumni, and fans have called for the locker room to be changed.

Whether the pink locker room is ultimately remembered fondly or in infamy, Hayden Fry's legacy remains there for all opponents who step into the visitors' locker room at Kinnick Stadium.

The Blackshirts
UNIVERSITY OF NEBRASKA

The tradition of Nebraska's Blackshirts was born out of necessity. The rule change in 1964 allowing for separate offensive and defensive teams meant that the Nebraska coaching staff needed an easy way to tell the two squads apart.

Various colors of pullover jerseys—like modern-day pinnies—were purchased to have the four squads wear over their practice jerseys: red for first-string offense, green for second-string offense, black for first-string defense, and gold for second-string defense.

The coaching staff decided to use the various color assignments to encourage the players to work hard to get on and stay on the first-string teams. The multicolor jerseys were given out at the beginning of each practice, rewarding players with a "better" color when they improved (or a "worse" one when they didn't). As Nebraska became known for its strong defensive performance, the first-string defense jerseys became a badge of honor.

Since that time, the tradition has evolved and so have the jerseys. Starting defense now earn their own personalized black Nebraska jerseys, indicating significant accomplishments among the elite Cornhusker defensive squad.

Additionally, the Blackshirts have adopted some pirate-like tendencies, and the defense will occasionally make an X across their chest emblematic of the skull and crossbones.

Ski-U-Mah
UNIVERSITY OF MINNESOTA

One of the oldest cheers in college football is Minnesota's "Ski-U-Mah," and it's pretty simple to learn. It's just a repeated chant of "Ski-U-Mah, Rah Rah Rah!"

Any Golden Gopher could tell you that Ski-U-Mah is pronounced SKY-YOU-MAH, and could also probably give you a quick history lesson on its origin. Back in 1884, two Minnesota rugby players named John Adams and Win Sargent created the cheer to rally the rugby team to victory. The cheer was popular and became used across the spectrum of the university's athletics programs.

Adams and Sargent stole the first part of Ski-U-Mah from the Sioux Native Americans, whose tribes live in Minnesota and other parts of the upper midwest, from Wisconsin to Montana. According to legend, the men overheard some Sioux boys yelling "Ski-Yoo" as they were racing canoes across Lake Pepin and misinterpreted their whoops of joy to mean the word "victory!"

The second part of Ski-U-Mah is just an abbreviation of University of Minnesota twisted so it rhymes with "rah." Together, the idea would be that their cheer would be a literal cry of "Victory for the University of Minnesota," but ultimately it's more "Yay for the University of Minnesota!"

Regardless of translational nuances, this inspiring battle cry is one for the history books.

Block I Card Stunts
UNIVERSITY OF ILLINOIS

The Fighting Illini have some of the most entertaining student fans in all of college football, and they've got the card stunts to prove it.

While card stunts at college football games may not have originated with the student population at Illinois, they've definitely created some of the best ones out there. At halftime of each home game, the Block I student section in Memorial Stadium turns the rest of the fans' heads when they work together to turn individual cardboard posters into giant animated pictures.

One of the most famous stunts that the Block I performs is their back-to-back beer mugs. Set on a bright orange background, the two giant mugs appear filled with a blue liquid—orange and blue being Illinois' colors. As the rest of the stadium chants, "Chug! Chug! Chug!" the two mugs look like they're draining rapidly.

Some of their other notable stunts have included Pac-Man eating an opponent's team logo, the words "Block I" and "Illini," and giant letter I's that quickly shift color from orange to blue and back to orange again.

The Block I is an organized bunch of superfans for which The Illini faithful and everyone else is grateful.

Breakfast Club
PURDUE UNIVERSITY

While many school's traditions happen right before or during football games, Purdue's best ritual happens hours before kickoff at the weekly convening of the Breakfast Club.

Early in the morning before each home game in West Lafayette, Indiana—even before tailgating starts—diehard Boilermakers fans head down to State Street for a tradition that's unlike any other. They don't look like Purdue fans because of their school-affiliated tees or sweatshirts, and they're not clad all in black and gold. Instead they're easily identified because they look like they're dressed for Halloween.

All up and down State Street, Purdue's most dedicated don their best costumes and get their fill of breakfast food and booze. They meander up and down the sidewalks between their favorite establishments and revel in the ridiculous.

It's not uncommon to see Pikachu and a ghostbuster enjoying beers with a cowboy and Uncle Sam, or a French maid and giant chicken scarfing down eggs alongside James Bond and a tiger. Often this party goes on for a few hours before people head over to tailgates, though some stick around State Street until it's time for the game to start.

Sooner Schooner
UNIVERSITY OF OKLAHOMA

The University of Oklahoma may be well known for its rallying cry of "Boomer Sooner!," but only the biggest Sooner fans know that Boomer and Sooner actually attend every home football game at Gaylord Family Memorial Stadium. That's because Boomer and Sooner are the names of the two ponies who pull the Sooner Schooner around.

The Sooner Schooner is a replica of a covered wagon that was donated to the university in the 1960s, and it became the official mascot of the Sooners in 1980. It's pulled by the two white ponies, Boomer and Sooner, after each time Oklahoma scores. The wagon and the ponies are under the care of the RUF/NEKS, the Sooner's all-male cheer squad.

Started in 1915 by a group of rambunctious Sooner athletics enthusiasts, the RUF/NEKs are the oldest all-male group of their kind in the country. For years they operated like a fraternity—complete with paddles—but are now under the auspices of the university's Athletic Department with other official school spirit organizations.

In 1973, LIL' SIS, their all-female counterpart was added, and together they care for the ponies and pilot the wagon at each game.

The Waving Song
OKLAHOMA STATE UNIVERSITY

In Oklahoma, it's not only the wheat that's waving, it's also the Oklahoma State football fans.

After the Cowboys score at Boone Pickens Stadium in Stillwater, Oklahoma, the crowd performs "The Waving Song," a tradition that dates back to 1908. The words are sung along to the tune of "In Old New York," and everyone at the game puts one arm up and waves it back and forth while singing the praises of Oklahoma State.

The song was first introduced to the Cowboys by Professor H. G. Seldombridge in 1908 as part of an Oklahoma State follies show that year. He'd originally heard it while on a trip to New York City to research theater selections for students to perform.

Professor Seldombridge found the song to be so catchy that he couldn't stop humming it when he returned from his trip. He decided it had to be the final number for the follies show he was planning, though once he mounted it on stage, the praises of New York City seemed out of place in Oklahoma. Lightning struck, and he immediately penned new words.

The new lyrics about Oklahoma State (then Oklahoma A&M College, or "OAMC") were so catchy that the students at the follies all stood up and sang along to encores of the song and added their own flair—the now-signature wave. More than a hundred years later Cowboys fans are still waving and praising the orange and black!

"Country Roads, Take Me Home"
WEST VIRGINIA UNIVERSITY

The connection between John Denver and West Virginia University might seem strange to any non-Mountaineer fan, but those who cheer for the gold and blue know that the love between the school and the country/folk singer is the real deal.

Back in 1971, after Denver released his hit song "Take Me Home, Country Roads," the song was played before each home game and after each West Virginia victory. This is because Denver describes the state as "almost heaven" in the lyrics of the song. And even though Denver is not an alumnus of WVU and never lived in the state, he felt the connection, too: he attended the dedication of Mountaineer Field after a series of renovations in 1980.

It's really quite a touching scene to watch—West Virginia has just beaten their opponents and all 60,000 fans in attendance at Mountaineer Field at Milan Puskar Stadium put their arms around one another's shoulders and sing together in unison, often drowning out the recording of John Denver that is pumping through the speakers.

Celebrating a victory like that is almost certainly heaven for Mountaineer fans.

"Wabash Cannonball"
KANSAS STATE UNIVERSITY

Before every game at Bill Snyder Family Stadium in Manhattan, Kansas, the Kansas State Wildcats go a little crazy to "Wabash Cannonball."

When the band turns to the student section and begins playing the opening lines of the song, the students go into a frenzy and quickly get into formation—The Wabash takes some good coordination and intuition on the part of Kansas State's students.

As the trombones herald the start of the dance, the students start clapping in rhythm and then start making eye contact with their neighbors. When the dancing starts, every other person in each row has to lean forward or backward, doing the opposite of the two people flanking them. This creates a rippling wave of purple and white as people inevitably get off rhythm or move in the wrong direction. General pandemonium breaks out as the band screams its way through each of the repeated verses until the final notes are played and the crowd shouts "K-S-U!"

The song appears to have been written as a tribute to transients riding trains in the late 1800s. Famous recordings were released in the 1930s by the Carter Family and Roy Acuff, though the song didn't reach Kansas State's campus in an official capacity until December of 1968, when it was played for a basketball game. All of the band's sheet music had been destroyed in a fire in the building housing the music department; that is, all music except for the "Wabash."

Ever since "Wabash Cannonball" survived that fire, Kansas State has been dancing along to the song in hopes it will bring similar good luck on the football field.

"Riff Ram"
TEXAS CHRISTIAN UNIVERSITY

"Riff Ram Bah Zoo
Lickety Lickety Zoo Zoo
Who Wah Wah Who
Give 'em Hell, TCU!"

These are the words to Texas Christian University's "Riff Ram" cheer, one of the weirdest and most unique cheers in all of college football. Most of the words are complete gibberish, but when shouted by an entire stadium of Horned Frogs fans, it can be downright intimidating.

Originally written for TCU back in the 1920s, the school has since updated the tradition a bit. Now, prior to each game, the cheer is chanted by fans captured in a video montage that plays on all the big screens at Amon G. Carter Stadium. The cheer repeats over and over while inspiring images of fans and players whizz by until finally it cuts briefly to black and a famous TCU alum or fan appears on the screen to chant the final "Give 'em Hell, TCU!"

Some of those famous alumni and fans have included MLB pitcher and Cy Young Award winner Jake Arrieta, *CBS Evening News* anchor Bob Schieffer, and country singer Brad Paisley.

"Hook 'em Horns"
UNIVERSITY OF TEXAS

November 11, 1955, is a day that will live in infamy for all Longhorns opponents: it's the day that the "Hook 'em Horns" hand gesture was first introduced at the University of Texas.

In 1955, the Head Yell Leader at Texas was Harley Clark, who was enthusiastic and innovative in his job. He was interested in bringing new traditions to the football games that year, including small megaphones for every student, funded by Old Gold Cigarettes, whose logo appeared on each plastic horn.

Harley also introduced the Hook 'em Horns gesture. It had been shown to him by his friend Henry Pitts, who thought it looked like their mascot. At the Friday pep rally later that week, he demonstrated to all the gathered students how to properly bend down their middle two fingers with their thumb and extend their outer two to make the gesture. He declared it the "official hand sign of the University of Texas," and it wasn't long before Hook 'em Horns caught fire; it's been around ever since.

The sign is so ubiquitous that the phrase "Hook 'em Horns" has become both a greeting and a farewell among the Longhorns faithful, much to the dismay of all their opponents. Both the gesture and the phrase for "Hook 'em Horns" have become the tradition that non-Texas fans love to hate.

But all those opponents should probably ask themselves whether they don't like "Hook 'em Horns" because they think it's dumb, or because they're just tired of losing to the Texas Longhorns!

The Masked Rider
TEXAS TECH UNIVERSITY

At the start of every home game at Texas Tech, the Red Raiders football team stands ready to run out onto the field and rile up their fans once their cue appears: the Masked Rider.

Like a gunshot, this imposing figure in a black mask, black hat, and red cape speeds across the field atop an intimidating all-black horse. With one arm raised, the rider whips the crowd into a frenzy as the horse careens down the field, clearing the way for the football team to sprint out.

This tradition started back in the 1930s but became an officially sanctioned event at The Gator Bowl on January 1, 1953, when Joe Kirk Fulton took the reins and charged across the field to lead out the Red Raiders before a stunned crowd. The crowd was so enthusiastic following Fulton's ride, and the effect was so impressive, that the university decided to implement the ride as a tradition.

After Fulton, a number of Texas Tech students have taken the mantle of the rider, though they were all men until 1974 when a young woman named Ann Fulton was chosen. Though the choice was considered controversial at the time, many women have since been given the honor to ride down the field.

The Baylor Line
BAYLOR UNIVERSITY

Freshmen at Baylor hold a very special place at college football games, and it's down on the field! At Baylor, the football team is preceded by a wave of freshman and first-year transfer students known as The Baylor Line.

Membership in this organization is open to all first-year Baylor students who can commit to being enthusiastic and present for home games. They all wear specialized yellow jerseys that contain the expected year of their graduation and a nickname on the back. Together they rush across the field at the start of each home game to create a tunnel through which the Baylor team enters. Leading the pack of first-year Baylor students are six leaders carrying flags that spell out B-A-Y-L-O-R.

The Baylor Line started in 1970 and is at the heart of creating spirit and excitement during Baylor football games. After the football team finishes their entrance onto the field, the Line retreats to their special section in the stadium—directly behind their opponents' bench. From there, The Baylor Line cheers on the Bears and taunts their unlucky opponents.

Waving the Wheat
UNIVERSITY OF KANSAS

One University of Kansas football tradition has an unknown origin, and to watch it happen is truly mesmerizing.

Jayhawks fans are constantly surrounded by wheat fields in Lawrence, Kansas, where KU is situated. Thus, it makes a lot of sense that one of the oldest athletics traditions at their school makes spectators feel like they're standing in the middle of a giant wheat field.

After important moments during football games—like after each touchdown—Jayhawks fans put both arms into the air and slowly wave them back and forth. This may be done with or without a unified rhythm, and sections and rows don't move uniformly in the same direction.

This seemingly haphazard structure to the waving of the wheat is by design, and the crowd inside Memorial Stadium actually looks like a field of wheat slowly waving in the Kansas breeze.

To stand inside all of those waving arms in the stadium is to know what it's like to be a single stalk of wheat in a much larger meadow, to be both an individual and part of a larger whole. And that's what it's like to be one voice in a chorus of fans cheering for the Jayhawks!

Sailgating in Husky Harbor
UNIVERSITY OF WASHINGTON

When your football stadium is built at the edge of a sizable body of water, some of your school's football traditions tend to a bit different than everyone else's. Such is the case for fans at the University of Washington, which is built at the edge of Lake Washington in Seattle.

Prior to football games at Husky Stadium, UW fans love to take in many of the same traditions that happen at campuses across the country: throwing a football around, listening to the school's marching band, and tailgating . . . only, Husky fans don't actually tailgate. They sail-gate.

Right at the edge of Lake Washington and Husky Stadium is a marina called Husky Harbor. Lots of UW fans park their own boats or rent out a charter for a sail-gating party. And what could be more fun? A good wind in the sails, tasty food on the grill, and a yacht underfoot all while preparing to watch the Huskies take to the field—that is living!

Leland Stanford Junior University Marching Band
STANFORD UNIVERSITY

Marching bands have done a lot of crazy things over the years, but the most offensive and irreverent marching band in all of college football is hands-down the Leland Stanford Junior University Marching Band.

Formed in 1963 after the regular marching band went on strike to protest the firing of their beloved director, Jules Schucat, the LSJUMB does not behave like any other college marching band. For starters, the band changes in size from performance to performance. They number their core group at roughly 30 participants, but for football games can field anywhere between 100 and 150 performers.

And their halftime shows are anything but typical. You won't find the LSJUMB marching in neat lines spelling out "Stanford" or "Cardinal." Rather, the band puts on elaborate musical skits that change each week. Their infamous "These Irish, Why Must They Fight?" halftime performance at a game against the Notre Dame Fighting Irish mocked the Catholic Church and the use of the Irish people as a combative mascot for the school and landed the band in some hot water. Thankfully, they survived mostly unscathed.

Often political, always very tongue-in-cheek, and never predictable, one thing that the Leland Stanford Junior University Marching Band can always guarantee Cardinal fans is a fantastic time.

Tightwad Hill
UNIVERSITY OF CALIFORNIA AT BERKELEY

Attendees of football games at UC Berkeley's Memorial Stadium may see a strange sight: football fans in lawn chairs and on blankets camped out on a hill that overlooks the stadium. These dedicated cheapskates are part of a nearly century-long tradition at Berkeley known as Tightwad Hill.

Because of the placement of Memorial Stadium, one of the most scenic places to watch sporting events has always been from the vantage point of Charter Hill, which offers views of the city of Berkeley, as well as San Francisco and the Bay in the distance. The fact that Cal Bears' fans can catch the games for free there is just an added bonus.

Tightwad Hill is considered to be part of the relaxed atmosphere on campus and in the surrounding city. Fans began gathering there to watch games back in 1923 when the stadium was first built, and have largely policed themselves in terms of sharing space and cleaning up after games. While disagreements certainly can crop up between fans sharing a limited space, Tightwad Hill's reputation is largely peaceful and communal.

In 2006, Tightwad Hill was under threat of elimination with a new stadium redesign, but a group of Golden Bears fans banded together to fight it in court. They won, and this strange tradition was preserved for future generations of Berkeley freeloaders.

Motorcycle Man
UNIVERSITY OF OREGON

The energy in Autzen Stadium is palpable just before the Oregon Ducks take the field in Eugene, Oregon. Fans are excited, the crowd cheers, and then comes the sound that everyone is waiting for: the rumble of a Harley revving up.

Leading the Ducks onto the field before every game is Motorcycle Man. For a long time, the mantle of Motorcycle Man has been held by Eugene local Doug Koke, who took it on after former Oregon and NFL player Gary Zimmerman. Sitting behind Motorcycle Man is The Duck, Oregon's costumed mascot, holding on to his driver with one arm and the American flag with the other.

The Harley they ride is a special motorcycle customized just for this purpose. Decked out in green and yellow with a special paint job, it is a sight to behold.

When the engine roars to life, the crowd at Autzen goes nuts. Then, as the motorcycle zooms down the field, engine blaring, American flag waving, and The Duck smiling, the football team and coaching staff make their entrance. It's game time!

Running with Ralphie
UNIVERSITY OF COLORADO

Lots of colleges have live mascots that attend their home football games, but none of them impresses quite like Ralphie, the University of Colorado Buffaloes mascot.

The first time a buffalo appeared at a Colorado football game was all the way back in 1934, but it just hung out on the sidelines in those early days. The first time Ralphie started running down the field was in 1967.

At the start of each half, five buffalo handlers and Ralphie take off across the football field and sprint around the field in a horseshoe pattern. It's an imposing sight—five students in jeans, black long-sleeve shirts, and black cowboy hats holding ropes attached to a harness around a giant, furry, brown buffalo. Together, they thunder down the field with the handlers guiding the buffalo to a pen at the opposite end.

Over the years, there have been five Ralphies at the University of Colorado, and all of them have been female because they're a little bit smaller and less aggressive than the males. Being one of Ralphie's handlers is a huge honor and responsibility. All interested Colorado students have to apply, undergo rigorous testing, and if selected have to dedicate at least thirty hours a week to Ralphie's care.

But it's worth it to be running alongside that gorgeous bison at each home game, inspiring the crowd while the football team trails behind you. It's a tradition that's thrilling, a little bit dangerous, and incredibly fun to witness.

Epic Pregame Show
UNIVERSITY OF SOUTHERN CALIFORNIA

Having a campus located close to the center of the filmmaking industry means that the expectations are high for production value and drama for any entertainment at campus sporting events. The pregame show that the University of Southern California puts on has all the flare of the Greek and Roman epic films of old Hollywood.

To begin this pregame, the drum major, dressed in his costume as a Trojan warrior, marches purposefully out to the center of the field. As he reaches his spot, standing in the center of the Los Angeles Memorial Coliseum, he performs some flashy moves with his bright-silver sword. He flips and flourishes it and then finally grabs the hilt and stabs it directly into the turf. The crowd roars wildly.

Then he conducts the marching band to join him out on the field and they slowly advance in their cardinal and gold uniforms while playing a stately fanfare. This song is called "Conquest," and it was originally written for the 1947 film *Captain from Castile*. The brassy fanfare has the feeling of a military march as it spurs the players and fans into battle against their opponents with the passion of ancient conquerors.

Crazy Lady
UNIVERSITY OF UTAH

Many college football fans take their love for their team to intervention-worthy levels of crazy, but at the University of Utah there is one crazy fan who is celebrated for her dedication to the team and to the art of dance.

The Crazy Lady tradition started back in 1983, when the marching band would play the theme from *The Blues Brothers* during the halftime celebration and an elderly woman nicknamed Bubbles would dance and shimmy energetically to the song in the stands. After this continued for a few home games to the stadium's delight, it became a tradition.

Bubbles continued her antics into the late 1990s, when she decided not to renew her season tickets. There was a bit of a void in her absence, and into that spot stepped another older woman named Terri Jackson, who assumed the mantle of the crazy, energetic woman who dances along to the marching band's *Blues Brothers* tribute. What started as a dance-off held by the band during the pregame tailgate turned into Jackson officially becoming part of the festivities during the third quarter of each game.

Beginning in 2000, Utes fans have been chanting for the Crazy Lady, and she's been dancing and shimmying her way into their hearts ever since.

Lantern Walk
ARIZONA STATE UNIVERSITY

Any college with a good football program has some really fantastic traditions in their Homecoming celebrations, and the Arizona State University Sun Devils are no different. They've got a really beautiful tradition that's been going on since 1917.

On the Friday before the homecoming game, ASU students, faculty, staff, and alumni all gather to hike up to the top of A Mountain, where the giant painted "A" reminds them of their Arizona pride. This hike takes place at night, and all of these Sun Devils make the climb lighted only by lanterns.

From a distance, the whole mountain appears lit up and the effect is truly special. Once everyone is gathered at the top, a few people speak, sharing rousing words about victory and teamwork and reminders of what's important to the ASU community. Then the homecoming court is announced, everyone celebrates their coronation, and the whole group heads back down the hill.

The Lantern Walk is a truly unique tradition and one that's visually stunning; a fitting reminder of how athletics and tradition can unite a community.

Barrel Man
UNIVERSITY OF WYOMING

Some college football fans are willing to give everything for their team—even their clothes! One University of Wyoming fan did exactly that for his beloved Cowboys.

Wyoming fan Ken Koretos started wearing a brown and gold barrel celebrating his favorite team back in the mid-90s after having a conversation with the famous Denver Broncos' Barrel Man, Tim McKernan. Their brief exchange inspired Koretos to bring that tradition from the NFL to the NCAA.

Since then, he's been showing up to every Wyoming home game in his cowboy hat, his cowboy boots, and his Cowboys barrel. He gets his fellow Wyoming fans riled up with his enthusiasm and cheers from the stands.

He's also a mainstay around tailgates. You'll find Barrel Man hanging out and having fun with other Cowboys fans before the game and giving all of the players big high fives as they make their way to the stadium on their gameday Cowboy Walk.

Barrel Man is an inspiration to fans everywhere willing to give it all for their teams.

Dollar Bills
UNITED STATES AIR FORCE ACADEMY

When it comes to showing their support for their team and the students at the Air Force Academy, fans in Colorado Springs do so with cold, hard cash.

Before each game starts at Falcon Stadium, the most dedicated fans get into the arena ahead of time to watch the band and the cadets process in and do formation drills on the field. These maneuvers are really impressive, quite similar to parade drills that happen prior to football games in Annapolis and West Point at the other US military academies.

What sets USAFA apart is that as the cadets and the band stand in the tunnel waiting to go out onto the field, Falcons fans will stand above them on either side of the tunnel and throw down one-dollar bills. Oftentimes, especially if the recipient is a member of the marching band, this monetary tribute will be followed by a shouted request for a song. However, requests for "Freebird" may not be honored.

This tradition is meant to bestow good luck on the cadets who receive the dollars. And Air Force cadets are truly lucky to have fans who'd give away their cash to give their favorite cadet some good fortune or to request a song from the marching band.

The Haka
UNIVERSITY OF HAWAI'I

Many college football teams attempt to intimidate their opponents through impressive displays of strength and teamwork. The University of Hawai'i Rainbow Warriors went as far as to reach back in their Polynesian roots to bring a war dance to Aloha Stadium for each home game.

The University of Hawai'i began performing the Haka after being inspired by the New Zealand All Blacks rugby team. The Haka has been performed before the start of the All Blacks' away matches since the late 1800s as a means of spreading traditional Maori customs around the world.

In 2006, native Hawai'ian Tala Esera introduced his Warriors teammates to the "Kapo O Pango," the Haka that was created specifically for the All Blacks, and they began to perform it before all of their home games to hype up the stadium crowd and intimidate their opponents.

However, due to issues with copyright infringement on the All Blacks' Haka and concerns about stealing from Maori culture, various team leaders have since brought in elements of the Hawai'ian Ha'a or added variations from other Haka dances to make the University of Hawai'i performance more specific to Hawai'i and to the Warriors.

This new tradition is evolving, but cultural sensitivity and a desire for Hawai'ian culture to be reflected in its university's football traditions keep driving the Warriors toward a dance that will inspire their fans and intimidate their opponents.

Running Down the Hill
CLEMSON UNIVERSITY

Most college football teams have a ritual surrounding their entrance into the stadium, and the Clemson Tigers are no different. Their entrance into Memorial Stadium in Clemson, South Carolina, is so exhilarating that sportscaster Brett Musberger dubbed it "the most exciting twenty-five seconds in college football" back in 1985.

The entrance into the stadium is fairly straightforward in execution—the Clemson players and coaching staff begin at the top of a hill and run down it into the stadium. But the experience of being there makes that simple description pale in comparison.

This entrance began out of necessity. After the stadium was constructed in 1942, the gate at the east end zone was the closest stadium entrance to the team's locker rooms at nearby Fike Field House.

Since then, the stadium has undergone renovations and locker rooms were built near the west end zone, but the tradition has remained intact many years later. Now the team leaves their locker room at the west end of the stadium and boards buses that take them around to the east end of the stadium, where the hill cuts a path through the seats in the end zone.

As the buses circle Memorial Stadium, Tiger's fans inside the arena cheer loudly. The sound reaches deafening levels as the team stands ready at the top of the hill; the noise is so loud that it's been measured at almost 133 decibels—the same sound level as a gunshot. Cannonfire booms and the team heads down the hill to the field, passing through a sea of Tiger fans, all in orange.

The Sod Cemetery
FLORIDA STATE UNIVERSITY

Many college football programs keep mementos from important victories, but the Florida State Seminoles take it to a whole other level—they steal part of their opponents' fields.

Back in October of 1962, Florida State dean Coyle Moore spoke to some of the team before they hit the road to play against Georgia, who was heavily favored to win the game. He gave the players some inspirational words and told them to bring back some of Georgia's field with them. When the underdog Seminoles defeated their opponents 18-0 that day, they took a chunk of the sod, brought it home to Dean Moore, and a small plaque was planted with the sod by the team's practice field.

Since then, anytime the Florida State Seminoles hit the road as the underdog team or for an important bowl game, if they come home victorious, a small piece of their opponent's grass comes home with the team and is planted by the practice field with a small plaque commemorating the win.

Since the tradition began in 1962, approximately 100 pieces of grass have been planted by the Seminoles' practice field, including wins against rival Florida, for ACC Championships, and National Championships. Every time Florida State's players walk onto their practice field, they can walk right over the grass of their vanquished foes of years past.

Class of the Finest
WAKE FOREST UNIVERSITY

At the final home game of the season at Wake Forest, underclassmen really show some respect for their elders: they throw a festive tailgate in celebration of the entire senior class called Class of the Finest.

Class of the Finest is held in a giant tent right near BB&T Field, and it features free food and drinks for any senior who wants to attend. Each year, it's organized by a committee of underclassmen, adding a communal feeling of gratitude for the senior class' years of service to the event.

This event is a rather new tradition for the Demon Deacons. Instituted in 2006, Class of the Finest was started as a direct reaction to an unofficial tradition that some Wake Forest seniors still celebrate under the radar: The Senior Fifth. During The Senior Fifth (which also takes place at the final home tailgate of the season) seniors attempt to drink an entire fifth of hard liquor before kickoff.

For most seniors at Wake Forest, Class of the Finest is a highlight of their final football season in Winston-Salem, North Carolina. They're surrounded by friends, good food, free drinks, and a fun day of football—there's nothing better.

Burning the Cleats
SYRACUSE UNIVERSITY

Fire can be a powerful tool for cleansing and sparking renewal. At Syracuse University in upstate New York, fire helps the football team mark the end of the season and a look toward the future.

During the 1980s, head coach Dick MacPherson started a tradition that at the conclusion of the football season, the Orange football players would start a fire and then toss in the cleats they'd worn all season. The tradition has continued since then, only stopping from 2005 to 2008 under head coach Greg Robinson.

This tradition helps the team feel a sense of finality about the work they put in each year. If the season ends with the Orange feeling disappointed about their performance, the fire provides the opportunity for the team to burn the bad and rebuild the following year. If the team played well, the fire can offer a celebration of a good season and a chance for teammates to come together and mark their victories.

Regardless of the season's outcome, this annual ritual provides a sense of unity for the Syracuse Orange, a chance to mark the end of another season in the books.

"The 'Hokie' Pokey"
VIRGINIA TECH

Between the third and fourth quarters of every home game, Virginia Tech Hokie fans perform a choreographed dance that many of them have been practicing since long before they donned the orange and maroon.

When the break happens between quarters, the tuba section of the Marching Virginians band heads out to the goal line of the end zone, backed up by the cheerleaders. The crowd cheers for the start of one of their favorite traditions: "The 'Hokie' Pokey."

When the song starts, the tuba section—all wearing their giant sousaphones—starts playing and doing a very energetic version of "The 'Hokie' Pokey." The crowd at Lane Stadium in Blacksburg joins in and delights in watching the roughly twenty giant sousaphones bouncing up and down and spinning around to a favorite song from childhood.

The tuba section performs the second-to-last verse as a solo while the rest of the band sits quietly. For the final verse, the tubas get really close together at the center of the goal line and start performing a kickline—all while playing and wearing their enormous instruments. That tuba section sure is fit!

The Smoke
UNIVERSITY OF MIAMI

When the Miami Hurricanes enter Hard Rock Stadium, they storm the field with a smoky flourish.

In a tradition that dates back to the 1950s, the 'Canes enter their home stadium in a steamy fashion thanks to Bob Nalette, the university's transportation director at the time. In hopes of stirring up more fan support and interest in the team, he decided to use fire extinguishers spraying through a system of pipes that he specially welded together to make the team's entrance more dramatic. In addition, Nalette added flashing lights, team flags, and the sound of hurricane-force winds pumped through the loudspeakers of the stadium.

Today the smoke entrance has evolved slightly. Instead of the lights and flags of yore, students, cheerleaders, the band, and other fans line the field in a makeshift tunnel, surrounded by smoke, as the team runs out to thunderous applause and the intense sound of howling winds plays.

It's an intimidating sight: a layer of smoke blankets the field, and emerging from underneath it come the Hurricanes charging in their bright-orange jerseys.

The Ramblin' Wreck
GEORGIA TECH

Like many other schools, Georgia Tech has more than one mascot attending its football games, though usually when this happens, it's a live animal and a costumed version of the same creature. At Georgia Tech's football games, there are two entirely different mascots: Buzz the Yellow Jacket and The Ramblin' Wreck.

The original Ramblin' Wreck was a car that belonged to college dean Floyd Field in the 1920s. Though it wasn't an official university mascot at the time, Dean Field's 1916 Model T was so beloved of the students that they named it The Ramblin' Wreck after the Georgia Tech fight song. The car's popularity led to an annual illegal—and dangerous—road race from Atlanta to Athens, Georgia, that was changed to a parade in 1932 at the behest of Dean Field himself. The Ramblin' Wreck Parade continues to this day during homecoming weekend.

The current Ramblin' Wreck—a 1930 Ford Model A—was a classic already when it was first brought to campus in 1961. It's a beautiful old car that's painted gold, has a very distinct horn, and is maintained by students in the Reck Club at Georgia Tech. At the start of each game, one student drives The Ramblin' Wreck through a paper banner with a few cheerleaders holding tight to each side, followed by the football team.

The Good Old Song
UNIVERSITY OF VIRGINIA

Every time that the Virginia Cavaliers score a touchdown, all the UVA fans put their arms around each other and start to sway. This isn't some sort of cult ritual, it's just "The Good Old Song."

"The Good Old Song" was written in 1893 and is sung to the melody of the classic New Year's ballad "Auld Lang Syne." Most of the words of the Virginia version are credited to Edward Craighill, Jr. (class of 1896), who insisted that the lyrics to the first stanza were written in collaboration with other students.

The song incorporates the strange phrase "wah hoo wah" into its lyrics multiple times, though no one is completely sure what the words mean or where they originated. It is thought that they were used as a cheer for the football team around the time that the lyrics were written by Craighill and his collaborators.

It's not actually an official university song, despite its popularity and longevity, though it's frequently mistaken to be the school's anthem by non-Cavaliers because of its frequent use at UVA gatherings and the tender way in which Cavaliers embrace one another when singing it.

Spirit Splash
UNIVERSITY OF CENTRAL FLORIDA

Central Florida can be a tough place to be a football fan with all the heat, humidity, and sunshine constantly beating down during the season. The students at the University of Central Florida have found that the best way to beat the heat is to host the homecoming week pep rally in a pool.

The shallow reflecting pool named "The Pond" that sits between Millican Hall and the John C. Hitt Library plays host to Spirit Splash each year. The students all gather around the edge of The Pond, and at the end of a countdown they all charge into the water to get the best spot to watch the pep rally. There's an appearance by Knightro the mascot, the pep band, cheer and dance squads, and some of the star Knights players come out to boost the crowd.

The origins of the first Spirit Splash are under dispute, but in either 1994 or 1995, a student-led initiative started the first party in The Pond. Whether you believe it was students gathering in The Pond to collect pennies for a Homecoming Week contest or the student government tossing in their president and following him in during the homecoming pep rally, everyone agrees that this is the most fun event at UCF.

A few years after Spirit Splash became an official campus event, someone thought up the idea to put rubber ducks in the pond, and now part of the mad dash after the countdown is to be one of the select few who gets a Spirit Splash duck.

Maybe it's not so tough to be a football fan in Central Florida. After all, that heat, humidity, and sunshine helped inspire the UCF Knights to throw one of the best parties in all of college football.

Bearcat Band Charge
UNIVERSITY OF CINCINNATI

There's a lot of dispute over which college football team has the most exciting or memorable entrance ritual at their home stadium. However, it's hard to dispute which band has the most exciting and memorable entrance to their home stadium after you've seen the Bearcat Band charge the field at the University of Cincinnati.

Before every home game, the percussion section takes their spot down on the field at Nippert Stadium, and an announcement comes over the speakers that it's time for the band to charge the field. From all corners of the bleachers comes the sound of a fanfare played by the remaining sections of the marching band.

The crowd of Bearcats fans gets to their feet and begins cheering wildly. Then, as the drums continue to thunder across the field, the music cuts out and the band runs down the steps of the stadium all the way to the turf in their bright-red uniforms. They stream into the center of the field from all sides and quickly get into formation.

The first Bearcat Band Charge happened in 1954 when band director Robert Hornyak decided they needed something new to increase interest in their performances. The members of his marching band were initially skeptical, but after practicing the charge and then performing it for an excited crowd, they were convinced. When stadium renovations meant a temporary move to nearby Paul Brown Stadium, home of the NFL Cincinnati Bengals, the band was the first to make sure that their tradition could continue in the new venue.

The Irish Guard
UNIVERSITY OF NOTRE DAME

As the Band of the Fighting Irish marches across campus on their way to each Saturday's home game at Notre Dame Stadium in South Bend, Indiana, they are led by a small group of tall students marching rigidly while clad in kilts, red military jackets, and very tall black hats. These imposing figures are the Irish Guard, members of the marching band and figures integral to much of the culture and traditions surrounding Notre Dame football.

The Irish Guard was formed in 1949 at the behest of band director H. Lee Hope, who wanted to add a new element to the band performances. Their uniforms and mannerisms were modeled after traditional Irish kilts and the Irish Guard regiment of the British Army. The plaid incorporated into their uniforms is a special Notre Dame tartan that was created by band director Robert O'Brien in 1966.

When they are not escorting the band around campus or standing by for outdoor performances before games, the Irish Guard is standing on the sidelines waiting for a touchdown. After each time that Notre Dame scores, the band strikes up the tune "Damsha Bua" and the Irish Guard performs a victory clog in the end zone to mark the score.

The Irish Guard is a special tradition at a school that is steeped in history and football culture. Just make sure not to be in front of the band when the Irish Guard comes through—true to their name, they will physically move anyone who is in the way of the band.

The Toast Toss
UNIVERSITY OF PENNSYLVANIA

"Drink a highball and be jolly / Here's a toast to dear old Penn!"

So go the words to "Drink a Highball," the song that all UPenn students and fans sing at the close of the third quarter of every home game at Franklin Field in Philadelphia. According to unsubstantiated legend, back in the day the entire student section would take the opportunity to actually drink a toast to their school during the final words of the song. That was until Franklin Field banned alcohol from the stadium in the 1970s.

The move to ban alcohol was obviously not without controversy, but students came up with an interesting way to vent their frustrations. When the line "Here's a toast to dear old Penn!" was sang, students who could no longer toast their alma mater with booze decided to instead salute her with literal toast.

Fairly soon, thousands of pieces of toast would rain down on the field from the student section at every home game, to the point that industrious engineering students created a toast "Zamboni" that can clear all of the carby goodness from the field before the fourth quarter starts.

The Toast Toss continues to this day at Franklin Field and perhaps stands as a warning to all who seek to quash the fun of college kids enjoying football. A group of students armed with an education and the desire to create mischief will find a way to do so.

RIVALRIES

The Game Pranks
HARVARD VS. YALE

Having first played each another in 1875, the football teams at Harvard and Yale share the oldest rivalry in college football. This contest is so revered that it's known simply as "The Game." While other football programs around the country have long dominated national championships, these two top academic institutions also focus their rivalry on other realms, including a series of pranks that have been nothing short of legendary.

One of the most notable high jinks occurred in 1933 when Harvard students—allegedly from *The Lampoon*—kidnapped Yale's bulldog mascot, Handsome Dan. Following Harvard's victory over Yale that year in The Game, the kidnappers smeared hamburger meat on the feet of the John Harvard statue on campus and published photographs of Handsome Dan licking the feet of their school's namesake.

One prank that's endured annually since the 1970s is the Saybrook Strip. At some point during The Game, a small group of Yale students who live in the dormitory Saybrook College will get as close to the field as they can and remove all of their clothing. Perhaps the most famous prank in recent years involved Yale students posing as Harvard students and convincing the Harvard fans at The Game in 2004 to perform a card stunt. Unbeknownst to the Harvard fans, the card stunt spelled out the words "WE SUCK" in bright red letters. The good-natured rivalry between these two academic powerhouses has provided the college football world with some very entertaining moments.

Game Week Antics
MICHIGAN VS. OHIO STATE

The rivalry between Michigan and Ohio State is one of the most famous in all of college sports. Two teams who field incredibly talented athletes, play competitively against one another, and have often competed for conference titles have plenty of ammo for a rivalry—which means that students and fans have had plenty of time to create some lasting traditions surrounding the games between these two titans.

In the week leading up to the annual game between Michigan and Ohio State, both teams have some late-night traditions.

At Ohio State, on the Thursday before the game against Michigan, students go out in the middle of the night to Mirror Lake and jump in. Mirror Lake is cold, and the late-season air is chilly in Columbus, Ohio. And yet many Ohio State faithful strip down to their bathing suits or their underwear and drench themselves to show their spirit.

Over in Ann Arbor, fans follow the coaching staff and some of the players out to Forest Hill Cemetery in the middle of the night to pay tribute to three men: former coach Bo Schembechler, former coach Fielding Yost, and longtime local radio broadcaster Bob Ufer. Sometimes trekking through the snow to visit the graves, those in attendance lay tokens and tributes on the graves of the men, once even smashing a buckeye nut on the grave of Bo Schembechler.

These crazy, late-night activities show what Michigan and Ohio State fans are made of: dedication and a willingness to do almost anything to show their hatred for each other.

The Iron Bowl
ALABAMA VS. AUBURN

The rivalry between Alabama and Auburn is perhaps the fiercest in all of college football. It divides families, makes neighbors into enemies, and has led to some very significant property destruction. All of that animosity stems from an annual tradition known as The Iron Bowl.

These two teams played each other annually from 1893 to 1907, at which point both teams refused to play over arguments concerning player compensation and the refs. It wasn't until 1948 that the two schools played each other again, and that was only because the Alabama state legislature passed a resolution that threatened to defund the schools if they continued to refuse to play each other.

Birmingham, Alabama, played host to the faceoff for many years as a neutral site, and the name of The Iron Bowl stems from Birmingham's prominence as an iron producer. However, in more recent years, the game has returned to the team's home stadiums, rotating back and forth between them each year.

Because Alabama has no professional sports teams, college and high school football remain the main sporting attraction for most Alabamians. With this rivalry being so intense, fans of either team love to use the game as an opportunity to brag about the win for a full year. Whether their battle cry is "Roll Tide" or "War Eagle," every football fan in Alabama is looking forward to the Iron Bowl.

"The World's Largest Outdoor Cocktail Party"
FLORIDA VS. GEORGIA

The rivalry between the University of Florida and the University of Georgia is fantastic both on and off the field. These two teams are often well-matched programs that put on a competitive game of quality college football. But it's the tailgate that the Gator and the Bulldog fans throw that is legendary.

The annual contest between these two teams has been held in the neutral location of Jacksonville, Florida, since 1933. Though the quality football between these two teams is a draw, the bigger draw might be the parties surrounding the annual game. Fans from both teams descend on Jacksonville for a four-day celebration of football, tailgating, and parties. The festivities are so epic that back in the 1950s, they earned the title "The World's Largest Outdoor Cocktail Party."

These days, the parties continue to impress. The organizers set up a whole section for RVers to have their own camp, there's a best-BBQ contest, and a ton of drinking, dancing, and partying. The leadership of both universities has tried to quell the partying side of the event in recent years, even going so far as to try to shut down the use of "The World's Largest Outdoor Cocktail Party" as the game's moniker.

However, if Bulldog and Gator fans have anything to say about it, their annual party in Jacksonville will rage on for many more years to come.

The Red River Run
OKLAHOMA VS. TEXAS

The annual matchup between the University of Oklahoma and the University of Texas each year is called The Red River Rivalry, taking place at the Cotton Bowl in Dallas, Texas. The game is always held on the second weekend of the Texas State Fair in October.

While the football at this game is often top-notch, one of the annual traditions that occurs in the days before the big game is an even bigger demonstration of athleticism, perseverance, and heart: The Red River Run.

The first Red River Run was held in 1983, when the ROTC programs from each school decided that they would run one game ball from their respective campuses to Dallas. It works out that each campus is just under 200 miles away from Dallas, so both teams of runners travel approximately the same distance to get to The Cotton Bowl. These young men and women run in staggered shifts—it's a tremendous testament to teamwork and the cooperative spirit of the armed forces.

In recent years, both ROTC programs have used The Red River Run as a chance to raise money for charity, and also started playing a touch football contest against each other at the Cotton Bowl once both game balls arrive.

There's a nice competitive camaraderie between the ROTC programs at UT and OU. While their alliances are to their own schools when it comes to athletics, they also acknowledge that at the conclusion of their four years in either Norman or Austin, they will work together afterward as officers in the armed forces.

The Jeweled Shillelagh
NOTRE DAME VS. USC

For thousands of years, Irish warriors carried long sticks fitted with a blunt stone at one end into battle. These traditional weapons, known as shillelaghs (*shi-lay-lees*) are like smaller, more agile maces, capable of inflicting serious damage. It's fitting that each year, the Notre Dame Fighting Irish and the USC Trojans battle for the right to a trophy modeled after one of these traditional clubs.

The rivalry dates back to Thanksgiving 1925 when USC's athletic director Gwynn Wilson and his wife, Marion, took a train to Lincoln, Nebraska, with a plan to convince famed Notre Dame coach Knute Rockne to schedule an annual game between the two schools. As the story goes, Wilson and his wife accompanied Rockne and his wife, Bonnie, back to South Bend on the train from Nebraska.

While Wilson failed to convince Rockne, Marion Wilson convinced Bonnie Rockne that the West Coast would be a nice escape in the middle of the South Bend winter. Bonnie Rockne in turn convinced her husband to foster the annual contest, and the first matchup was scheduled for the following season.

In 1952, the Notre Dame Alumni Club of Los Angeles donated a shillelagh to be used as a trophy for the annual contest. Each year a gold insignia of the winner would be added to the handle of the club to mark the victory. This first one—The Jeweled Shillelagh—was filled by 1989 and the LA Alumni donated a new one. Each year, the winner of their annual matchup is awarded with the trophy and retains it for the full year. The original Jeweled Shillelagh is permanently displayed at Notre Dame.

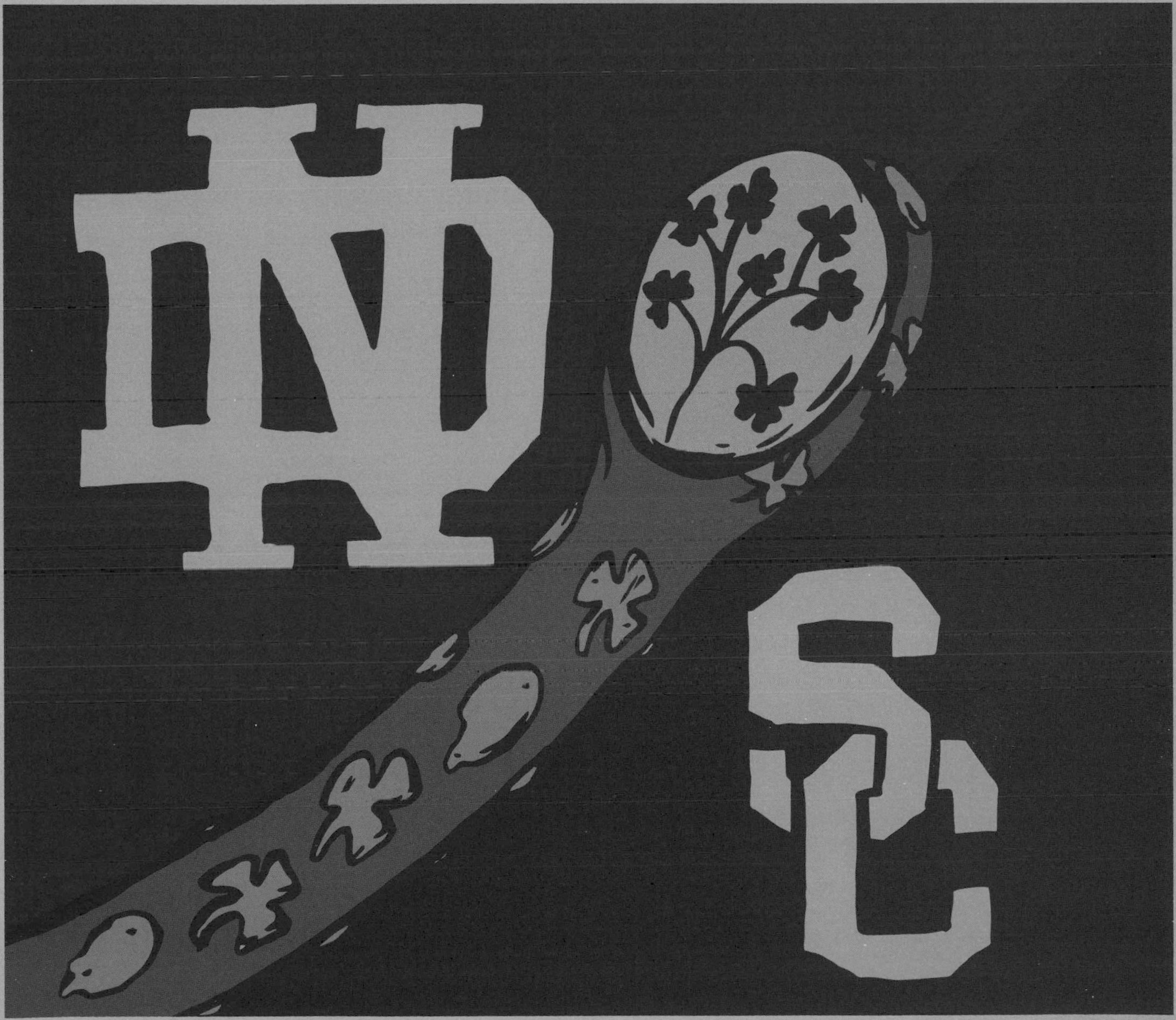

Brothers in Arms
ARMY VS. NAVY

One of the most anticipated matchups in college football each year is the annual Army-Navy game. It's often scheduled as the final regular season contest in all of Division I football, and has mostly taken place in Philadelphia over the years.

These two teams have a deep history of shared traditions. After each team scores at their home games, students perform push-ups down on the field. Many colleges have push-up traditions, but Army and Navy are special in that regular students, cheerleaders, and mascots do push-ups on the field.

Each academy also performs traditional military parade exercises before home games. At West Point, Army Cadets do these exercises on the The Plain three hours before kickoff, while in Annapolis, the Midshipmen do theirs on the field at Navy-Marine Corps Memorial Stadium just prior to kickoff. For the annual Army-Navy contest, each academy performs the march-on in coordination, sharing the field space cooperatively to run their parade drills a few hours before the game starts.

After the march-on concludes, select Cadets and Midshipmen who have spent the fall semester of their junior years at the rival academy are "given back" to their home academy. This "prisoner exchange" allows the juniors to cheer on their home team with their fellow classmen.

At the conclusion of the annual game, players from both teams gather together in the center of the field and sing the alma maters of each school to the gathered crowd.

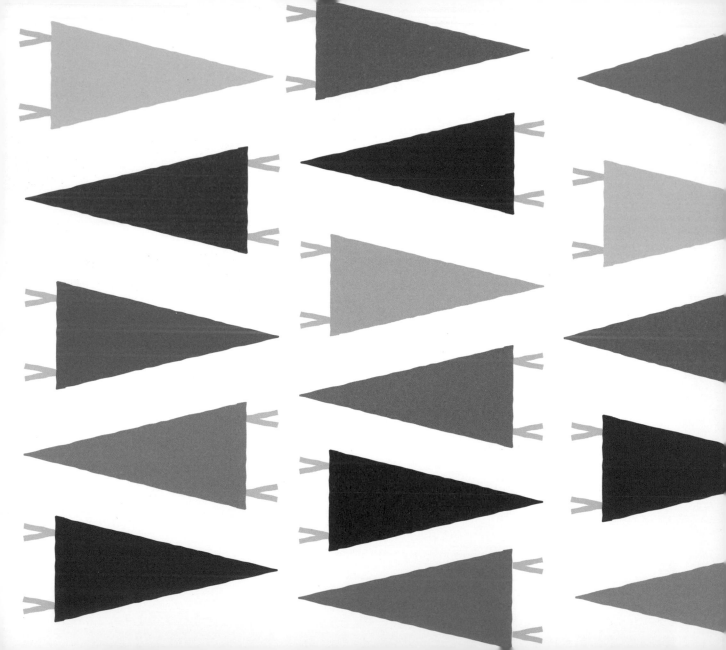

BONUS POINTS

We tried to capture as many college football traditions as possible, but there are plenty out there that we didn't cover. Here's a quick list of a few others that are worth checking out:

The Purple Clock
Northwestern University

After every Northwestern victory, the clock tower atop the Rebecca Crown Center changes to bright purple in honor of the university's colors.

"The Law of the Jungle"
University of Nevada

Before each Wolf Pack home game, the students and other loyal fans join together to chant "The Law of the Jungle" from Rudyard Kipling's *The Jungle Book*.

Purple Haze
East Carolina University

The East Carolina Panthers storm the field in a cloud of purple smoke, representing their team color, while Jimi Hendrix's song "Purple Haze" plays over the stadium speakers.

Boulevarding
Southern Methodist University

SMU doesn't tailgate—they boulevard! Mustangs football festivities take place along Bishop's Boulevard, which runs through the heart of campus and lends its name to SMU's specific brand of pre-gaming.

"Sweet Caroline"
Iowa State University

Between the third and fourth quarter, the student section leads a stadium singalong of Neil Diamond's "Sweet Caroline," similar to the long-standing tradition at Fenway Park, home of the Boston Red Sox.

The Blue
Boise State University

The turf at Boise State's Albertsons Stadium is bright blue instead of the standard green, so the field is commonly referred to as "The Blue."

Comatose the Cannon
Colorado State University

Colorado State has been firing off a cannon during the National Anthem, at opening kickoff, and after each CSU score since 1920.

"The Scotsman"
Utah State University

"The Scotsman" was written by Ebenezer Kirkham (Utah State class of 1918), had hand movements added to it by students in the 1990s, and is sung during football games, typically after the fight song "Hail the Utah Aggies."

Ramases the Ram
University of North Carolina

Though they've long had the nickname "The Tar Heels," UNC students felt they needed a mascot, so they bought a ram—a choice inspired by former NC fullback Jack Merrit, who was nicknamed "The Battering Ram."

"Bear Down"
University of Arizona

The phrase "Bear Down" has been a rallying cry at Arizona for many years, dating back to the tragic death of quarterback John Button Salmon, who told his coach J. F. McKale "Tell the team to bear down" after getting critically hurt in an automobile accident in 1926.

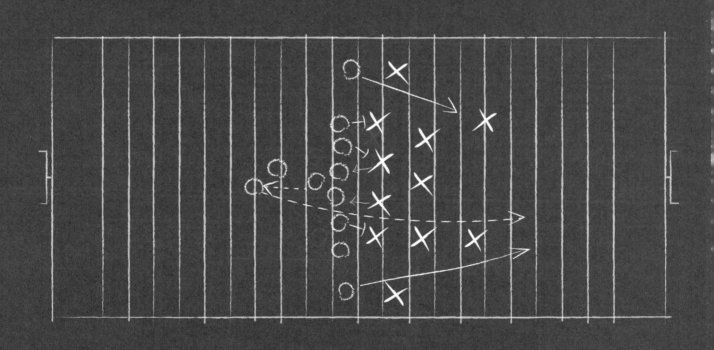